Ulrike Laubner

Katharina Brunner | Frank Lemser | Eduardo Lopes

Powerful communication
for product managers

Set the stage for reliable market facts and
successful collaboration

Bibliographic information from the German National Library
(*Deutsche Nationalbibliothek*):
The German National Library (*Deutsche Nationalbibliothek*) has
listed this publication in the German National Bibliography
(*Deutschen Nationalbibliographie*); detailed bibliographic
information can be found online at http://dnb.d-nb.de.

© October 2018, First edition
Production and publisher: BoD – Books on Demand,
Norderstedt. ISBN: 9783752855050

Layout: Ulrike Laubner
Graphics: Ulrike Laubner, Eduardo Lopes, Katharina Brunner
Icon: iconmastr
Cover design: Guter Punkt, Munich | iStock
Translation: Lingua-World, Germany

Foreword

Both companies and HR consultants consider communication to be the most important social skill for the future. For you as a product manager, good communication skills are decisive, both for your career and to ensure that you deliver a successful product. Yet we often still hear complaints about communication not functioning well with other departments and about the lack of acceptance of product management in many companies.

Using examples from the real world of business, this unique self-help guide looks at the typical communication difficulties which often arise and highlights potential solutions. There are also several exercises for you to test your new knowledge. The communication skills you acquire will simplify your everyday working life:

- You will improve your communication skills.
- You will learn how to convey information more effectively and how to convince stakeholders of your ideas.
- You will enhance your ability to pose tactical questions in order to increase your knowledge of the market.
- You will build up skills which will enable you to deliver customer-focused product management.

Your company will benefit in different ways – senior management will be able to make decisions faster and development teams will be able to carry out their development work according to real market requirements. In addition, the sales team will find selling easier and employees will get more enjoyment out of their work.

I wish you every success in putting these ideas into practice. You will soon find you are experiencing more acceptance from the various departments you deal with.

About the author

Ulrike Laubner is an expert in product management. She has a profound knowledge of the value which product managers generate for a company, having herself spent time working as a product manager and in other leadership roles in various international companies. She understands the challenges involved in communications and knows what it is like to come up against internal hurdle. She has experienced this situation herself. Her methods of improving communication skills are very convincing on account of both their ability to be implemented quickly and the visibility of the success they bring about. The information which provides the basis for her knowledge has been collected from a range of companies and industries and she has worked with the methods herself.

She enables companies and employees to develop their expertise in product management through certified training courses, workshops and consultancy. Companies and product managers achieve a noticeable improvement in collaboration and are able to launch new products onto the market faster through systematic product management and effective methods of communication.

As a member of the international non-profit organisation 'Toastmasters', she coaches and trains other members. Through this initiative, Ulrike Laubner provides training in communication and management skills which they can use in both their private and their professional environments.

In this practice-based self-help guide, she has summarised her findings on communication at the interfaces of product management, as well as her experiences as a coach, consultant, speaker, manager and lecturer.

About the co-authors

Katharina Brunner
Katharina Brunner spent 20 years working with considerable success in the field of corporate communications for number of companies, based both in Germany and further afield, before setting up her own consultancy focusing on user experience in 2014. She had already laid the foundations for this with her degree in Journalism and Communication Studies. With her company Maevis Consulting, which is based in Zurich, she advises companies who want to make user-friendly and successful products on improving the interfaces between product management, IT and marketing.

Eduardo Lopes
Eduardo Lopes has been working as a product, marketing and project manager in the engineering and connectivity industries since the year 2010. His style of product management is distinguished by products which create value as well as by a rapid time-to-market. For his Bachelor thesis, he carried out an in-depth investigation into the subject of product launches in the B2B market.

Frank Lemser
Frank Lemser is a Business Engineer and has been involved with his passionate interest, product management, since the year 2000, in both practical and academic terms.
As Managing Director of and coach for proProduktmanagement GmbH, he trains and issues certification to product managers according to Open Product Management Workflow™. He developed Open Product Management Workflow™ and its tools for product management in order to simplify collaboration with other departments, thereby saving valuable time for all those involved. He is regularly faced by new challenges in his training and consultancy sessions and succeeds in providing solutions for profitable product management.

Acknowledgments

I would like to thank all the product managers who have spoken openly to me about their difficulties. Without their input, it would not have been possible for me to write this book. My special thanks go to Meike Diesing, Jana Sachtleben-Wochnik, Gudrun Houry and Jenna Olejiczak for their support of this book.

Contents

Inhalt

Quick transfer exercises

"The art of communicating with one another
properly is like learning to walk –
you keep falling over, again and again,
until finally someone kindly takes you by the
hand."
(Wilma Eudenbach)

I. SPEAKING AND PRESENTATION SKILLS

1.   The four styles of communication

Imagine the following situation – you are talking to your manager and he keeps looking at his watch and tapping his foot. Then he says, 'Could you maybe get to the point?" How does that make you feel?

Try not to take it personally when someone behaves likes this or in any other particular way. You don't know what personal 'baggage' they are carrying around with them. Stress because of the traffic, a sick child or a divorce, a win on the lottery or approaching holidays – all these factors may influence the course of a conversation or on the atmosphere.

Yet it is irrelevant what situation people happen to find themselves in, because communication styles are dependent on the personality of the individual in question. When you have recognised this fact, then you will react appropriately, and you will make efficient use of both your time and that of the person you are talking to.

"If you want to have an effect on others, then you first of all need to speak to them in their own language" (Kurt Tucholsky)

Speak the language of the person you are talking to and in doing so avoid frustration, misunderstandings and the necessity for further meetings with more presentations to clarify things that were not made clear. The following table gives you an overview of four typical styles of communication and the best way to react to them:

Table 1: Styles of communication and how to deal with them

Type	Style of communication	How to deal with it
direct	resolute manner of speaking, formal, speaks loud and quickly, direct eye contact, firm handshake, keeps distance	good preparation, be well-informed on the facts, summarise content, pose direct questions, tend towards being formal, assume an upright posture
lively	tends to generalise, convincing manner, gives their opinion, acts fast, moves a lot, speaks loud, assertive handshake, a lot of variation in mood	listen to their experience, integrate them into finding solutions, state time available, deliver entertaining information, allow time for discussion, keep eye contact
calm	good listener, uses personal language, a lot of gestures, speaks and moves slowly, gentle handshake, gives verbal support	allow time to get to know one another and for personal matters, address common issues, be relaxed, create an atmosphere of trust for expressing personal opinions
systematic	focussed on details, expresses themselves in brief sentences, little variation in mood, controlled movements, not much emotion	focus on facts and figures, define the structure, e.g. time, content, measurement criteria, ask targeted questions about details, don't speak or move too quickly or in too hectic a manner.

Did you recognise your own style of communication? You will find these different styles of communication or combinations of them everywhere, and you will find yourself in one of them too. There are no good or bad styles of communication – each of them has its place and its specific strengths and weaknesses. If you want to learn how to recognise these different styles of communication, then start in your own surroundings. You can practise every day and you will get better at it; for example, small talk on the bus or on the train, conversation with friends or colleagues at work, with your partner and your children.

2. Ego Marketing – Product Managers are important

As the person responsible for a product, you are in fact presenting your company when you interview customers, talk to visitors at trade fairs or carry out product training. Your presence is of key importance when you take part in management meetings or lead kick-off meetings. You carry responsibility for the future of the company and the success of the product. You are important. You are in the spotlight, whether you like it or not. Do you know the impact you have when you are standing in the spotlight? Are you aware of your strengths and are you confident?

If you catch yourself asking yourself the following questions every now and then, then you can find methods in this chapter to strengthen your self-confidence as a product manager and to help you to present your knowledge.

- How come Ms Miller is getting a pay rise again?
- How is it that Mr Owen always manages to transform his innovative ideas into projects?
- How come the others are allowed to travel abroad to visit their customers again, and not me?
- Why is it always the others who get the interesting products?
- Why didn't I get a promotion this year?

A healthy dose of self-marketing is a strong means of success. Don't let yourself believe otherwise, as most people will be full of admiration for your self-confidence. Those people are of course to be distinguished from those who have narcissistic tendencies and always exaggerate their achievements - which are often quite mediocre - and broadcast them to the whole world.

It has become clear to me that, in many different companies and industries, self-marketing is a difficult theme for women in particular. Men seem to learn this skill from a very early age and enjoy telling people what they have achieved or have done well. Women tend to assign successes to other people and don't like to advertise their good performance. Yet they often ask themselves why they and their achievements are being overlooked.

It's quite simple – when we look up at the night sky, the first thing we see is the stars that are shining the brightest.

Your motto therefore needs to be 'DO THINGS WELL AND TALK ABOUT IT' and you will experience what Henry Ford once told us:

"Ducks lay their eggs in complete silence. Hens cluck like crazy when they are laying. What is the result? Everyone in the world eats hens' eggs. "

Self-marketing is necessary for good relationships and for your career. Consider for a moment it is you, who wants to ask somebody for advice. Who would you go to? Those who you trust on the basis of their knowledge and experience. Am I correct? Start sharing your achievements now.

If you invest time in marketing your ego, then you will progress further in product management, you will earn more, and you will be given the more   interesting product ranges to work with. You will also be given greater freedom in the way you organise your work. So much for the advantages.

The disadvantage may be that some people become envious of you. But this will be meaningless to you as you are pursuing your goals through honest means.

Think about it – people are only envious of those who are successful! A couple of quotes from my own career – "Ulrike, how come you got the job?" "How can the management trust you after such a short time, when I've been on the job for six years?", "I don't think it's fair that you are allowed, repeatedly to travel abroad for long periods of time."

In this chapter, you will learn some tactical methods of telling others about your achievements, without needing to change your basic character. You don't need to copy anyone – you are good as you are! It will take you around 15 minutes to note down the answers to the following questions:

1. Which tasks are you good at dealing with?
2. Which tasks have resulted in you getting positive feedback?
3. Can you think of any stories which would demonstrate your success?
4. Which people are important for your career?

If you become aware of your successes, then you will also want to tell people about them. You will then find to become more self-confident. Examples of market places for ego marketing:

- Employee events
- Speeches and presentations
- Project kick-offs and roll-outs
- Strategy meetings
- Articles in company magazines/intranet/blogs
- Conversations with employees
- Conversations with your superiors

Your homework for your own self-marketing:
1. Write down some of your success stories and learn to
2. tell them in an effective way.
3. Choose your market places for self-marketing.
4. Set deadlines in your diary for your own self-marketing campaigns, e.g. "Write down two success stories by 20 Oct" or "Give a talk or presentation at the next company event."

In the next chapter, you will find out how to give effective presentations.

3.   5 'Hot seasoning techniques' for more spice and increased effectiveness

Would you like to improve the way you market yourself or are you thinking of applying for a new job? Would you like to sell a new product to your senior management or organise a training session for employees? Then you will need to communicate in a clear and concise manner. In this context, remembering the phrase 'less is more" can be very powerful.

Recently, on a train journey, a product manager told me he felt that presentations for new products were 'too brightly-coloured and overloaded, no one understands them. Except the presenter!' Often times the main focus is lost with overly creative PowerPoints.

Necessary items of information get lost in mere empty noise. There is no doubt that information on technical details is important if your goal is to train technical support staff. However, if you are trying to sell an idea or concept for a product internally, then you need to use words that hit the mark the first time around. This means using content that is easy to understand and remember. Make sure to present the benefits for the customers in a self-assured manner.

 Think about yourself. When are you more likely to believe the content that another person is selling?

- when you have understood the content?
- when you have faith in the experience of the speaker?
- when the arguments are presented in a logical fashion?

You don't need to be a brilliant speaker to win over your colleagues and managers. There are effective methods of becoming a convincing speaker which are easy to learn. I call these methods my 'HOT SEASONING TECHNIQUES'.

1. Speak in the first person

The following sentence is typical of many presentations – "The new machine has eight innovative features and has been built on the basis of our new standard. If you take into consideration the fact that our new 'Airflow' technology is also more sustainable and uses fewer raw materials, then this innovation will revolutionise the market."

Hello? Hello! Have you fallen asleep?

What do you think about the following sentence? – "I carried out an investigation of the market from July to September and I established that 85% of potential customers had issues with recycled PET. They reported high costs in terms of warehouse administration. The customers told me that, since the introduction of the recycling system, their warehousing costs had gone up by 40%. And these are costs which they can only rarely recoup from their products. With the XXX technology, we are helping our customers to make a 60% saving in current processing costs. I have also carried out an analysis of our competitors and have established that none of them have the expertise to manufacture this material for themselves in the near future. I would like to present this innovation to you with eight new functions."

2. Involve the listeners

I'm sure you have been in this situation – you are listening to a 20 to 45-minute talk and you find yourself gently drifting off, or perhaps you send off a text message or two. I presume you don't want to experience this when you are the speaker.

Speak directly to your audience. That should be very easy in your own company as you know the listeners, their roles and their way of thinking. Use this to build language bridges between your content and the listeners. If they feel you are addressing them directly, they will remain fully focused on what you are saying.

Use interaction to keep the attention of your listeners. You can achieve this by using rhetorical questions, votes or surveys, as the following examples show:

"Ms Bright, I have heard from your customers that …"

"What solution do you think the competition has in mind for its customers?"

"If you had to make a decision, who would go for solution A? Please raise your hand."

With the last example of interaction, it is important that you raise your hand yourself, because the listeners will then do the same. This also makes it easier for you to count the votes.

3. Use words with impact

Experts and people who are passionate about what they do often run on with their sentences. Yet in verbal communication, this is often toxic as the next example will show – "In andragogy, we apply multiple different learning methods which the lecturer combines for the students by means of classical learning methods, blended learning and various different types of media and theoretical learning focuses." Listening to this kind of thing is not much fun!

However, if you use words with impact, you will have your listeners hanging on every word:

Eliminate words which have no added value
- but
- actually
- certainly/really
- generally speaking
- I believe/think/hope

They don't provide any additional information and they weaken your content. Shorten sentences which have two or three instances of 'and' or 'and that' by creating two or three shorter sentences.

Use words that address all our senses

Listeners can relate better to what is being said if all five senses are addressed – sight, hearing, smell, touch and taste. These experiences stay in our memories, as they are perceived by our brains in a more direct way. Spice up your stories with 'sensory statements'. This can work with technical products too – after all, a polished stainless-steel surface is smooth and cool, the new visual line gives it a softer feel and takes away any feeling of aggression, and the new material feels silky smooth.

Use specific descriptions

Say goodbye to empty phrases. Instead of "We are the technology leaders in…", your content will become more tangible and more interesting for the listener if you formulate your sentences as follows – "We are the Number 1 for fork lift trucks. We achieve 80% of our sales revenues with …"

Make use of pauses

Pauses are another important way of adding a bit of spice and are all too often underestimated in their importance. Pauses allow you to draw breath and give you time to reflect; they can also help to achieve a feeling of suspense or add a bit of humour. Your listeners will be grateful to you for a few breaks which allow them time to fully digest jokes, figures and facts or new concepts.

Here are a few instances where you should try to provide longer pauses:

- when there is a change of the line of thought or theme (1 second)
- when you have just finished telling a joke (3 - 5 seconds)
- when you use gestures to underline something you have said
- after rhetorical questions (2 seconds)

Repetition emphasises importance

'Anaphora' is a rhetorical stylistic device which you can use to emphasise the importance of certain themes or features. 'Anaphora' is a rhetorical stylistic device which you can use as a manager when you want to demonstrate something important to your staff or you want to ensure that important product features are fixed in your customers' minds.

'Anaphora' is a rhetorical stylistic device which you will be familiar with from recent political history – "Yes, we can!" as Barack Obama said.

'Anaphora' is a rhetorical stylistic device which involves repeating the same words in several consecutive sentences in order to focus attention on a theme, a product feature or a new concept. You will achieve maximum attention by repeating the word four times. I bet you will never forget that anaphora is a rhetorical stylistic device …!

4.   Avoid using complicated phrases

In the first example, a number of listeners will not have known what 'andragogy' or 'blended learning' mean. They will have asked their neighbour or googled in their phones to find an answer. The speaker lost their attention and they stopped listening. It is therefore your task to give some consideration to who the participants are going to be and what level of previous knowledge they will be bringing with them. You can then select a suitable level of language for your audience.

Avoid using complicated or foreign words or phrases and say what you really mean, e.g.:

- andragogy = methods used in adult education
- blended learning = courses where part of the teaching is done online

5.   Let figures do the talking

If you are trying to sell a product idea internally, you are asking your management to spend money. The management will want to know what they will be receiving in return. Here are some useful sources of such information:

- facts from customer interviews
- CRM and ERP systems
- performance indicators

- comparisons with the past or with competitors
- other industries
- trend analyses, etc.

Be creative and present the information in a simple way which is realistic in terms of actual figures. Figures can impress people, but it is possible you may be measured against them. It is not advisable to make a positive exaggeration, for example, when you are estimating the revenue figures for the next three years or giving an indication of market potential.

Here is an exercise for you to practise effective speaking:
Record a short presentation using your phone or laptop and then listen to it.
Rewrite the text of your presentation according to the 'hot seasoning techniques'. Eliminate all words that are 'stumbling blocks' for you and record the presentation again.
What differences do you notice?

4.   SERVIS – The listener is your customer

First of all, I would like to tell you a story. I received a request from a customer to give a talk. I am talking about a paid talk. And I mean really well paid! There would be 150 unknown pairs of ears waiting to hear what I had to say. 98% of them men from technical areas of work. I was to have 45 minutes to get across my message to them. There I stood, the first speaker on the programme, after the eloquent company directors had said their piece. The only female speaker, I was standing there on a podium as large as a theatre stage. I talked about products which don't sell well and those which are introduced onto the market too late. I spoke about the consequences for the company. Of course, I then went on to highlight the recipe for success for fast product development which at the same time conserves resources. For 50 minutes, I stared out across a sea of faces which were all turned towards me. Smiles and nods of approval. And then something amazing happened – I received the first round of spontaneous applause. My preparation had paid off.

Why is it that some product managers fall at the first gate when they are giving a presentation, while other speakers keep us rapt right to the last word? As a product manager, you want to fill people with enthusiasm and convince them of your ideas or a new product. This means that it is up to you to find words, pictures, stories and arguments that your listeners will understand. The worm needs to taste good for the fish and not for the fisherman. Why would the fisherman otherwise choose these slimy, wriggly larvae as bait? The larvae don't suit our taste buds, but for the fish they are an absolute gourmet dish. Make the content of your talk taste good for your listeners. The content needs to appeal to them.

That's why I developed the 'SERVIS' sales process. It is intended to show you the best possible way to get prepared for your customers or your colleagues. Depending on how well you know the listeners, your preparation may take anything from a few minutes for an internal presentation to several hours for a talk being given at an association meeting, for example, where the audience will be unfamiliar to you.

1.   Structure

Every talk or presentation has a goal. You may be aiming to inform people, to motivate them or to convince them of something. Without having a goal, a talk, presentation or even a negotiation session can become confused and people will find it difficult to follow your line of thinking. Let's take a look at the following example - In the course of a coaching session on presentations, I listened to a talk entitled 'Big Data'. I heard phrases such as 'Industry 5.0', ' Appliances', 'SQL','OTPS' taken from various technical papers and, after seven minutes, I asked my client, "What am I supposed to have understood from your presentation?" The reply – "I wanted to tell you about the opportunities and risks of Big Data and explain what is currently going on in this area." Strange. I had the feeling he wanted to turn me into a database specialist.

Before you start your presentation, define the goal that you are aiming at, and structure your presentation according to this goal – introduction, main part with sub-sections and a conclusion with a clear appeal to the listeners, telling them what they should do now.

When you start the presentation, tell the listeners what your goal is, so that it is easier for them to follow.

2.   Empathy

It is important to try and put yourself in your listeners' shoes so that you will be able to find the right words and pictures to use. And if you don't know who the listeners are going to be? Then ask your manager, or the organiser of the event, or take a moment to consider who might be taking part in the meeting and collect as much information as you feel is required. By telling personal stories which refer to the theme in question and citing similar experiences to those of your listeners, you will come very close to being in their world. If you have sold your story well, then you will have gained credibility and earned the trust of your listeners. You will have shown that you have understood the feelings, needs and circumstances of the audience. You are one of them!

3.   Recipes

Now you need to prepare the content of your talk or presentation. You will gain the attention of the listeners if you tell them something that that will bring them personal success or will help them to see an improvement in their own lives. **Solutions which make their lives more enjoyable or enhance success:** Relaxation, health, higher margins, higher sales figures, status, earning more money.

Solutions which allow them to avoid pain or frustration
Being able to sell ideas more easily, convincing children of ideas, asserting yourself to gain an increase in salary, making car repairs easier, losing weight, new sales markets, new

customer groups.
In business situations, the basis here needs to be a question of saving time or money if you are to retain the attention of the listeners and financiers.

Solutions which save time
Reduction in development time, new machinery, faster delivery times, automatic evaluation of business data.

Solutions which save money
Reduction in marketing costs, shorter processes, reduction in man hours, increase in performance of equipment, more expertise.

The benefits are best communicated through success stories with positive case studies or demonstrations which the listeners can relate to personally. You can garnish and therefore strengthen your story through the use of emotion-laden words. You can find a selection of emotion-laden words online, e.g. at: https://www.thepersuasionrevolution.com/380-high-emotion-persuasive-words/

4. Vetos
The listeners at a meeting, a sales conference or a product training session are busy checking their phones, posting messages on Facebook, whispering to their neighbours or frowning and giving you critical looks.
How can this be happening? After all, you are a relatively experienced speaker and have prepared your talk well.
It may be that the listeners don't actually understand your line of thought or your argumentation! If you notice this happening, then a sense of resentment will usually start to build up, and this will in turn be reflected in your facial expressions and your gestures.

Try to pick up on any resistance to your content in advance:

- What previous experience have the listeners perhaps had which could lead to them not trusting me?
- What worries or fears might arise?
- What controversial opinions are currently circulating on this theme in the industry/media/society?

Write down the answers to the above and incorporate your findings into your talk or into the conversation, and always keep an extra joker in reserve so that you can react to unexpected vetoes.

5. Information

Tastes vary when it comes to food and wine, and the same applies to presentation styles. Some people like messages to be succinctly brought to the point, others like a bit of humour, and others again prefer to be provided with technical details.
In order to prepare your information in a listener-friendly way, ask yourself the following questions before the presentation:

- What kind of language should I use? Formal, casual, specialist terminology?
- What are the current general circumstances of the listeners?
- What experience and background do the listeners have?
- What experience do you have in common with the listeners?

 Take ten minutes to try out the following exercise:
You want to motivate your customers to use only two-ply toilet paper in their company in future. What kind of words would you use in terms of your arguments, your emotions and the stories you tell for the following groups of listeners?

- Women
- Men

23

- Mixed groups
- Manufacturers of toilet paper and company bosses

Can you see the difference? Great, then you have succeeded in putting the SERVIS strategy into practice.

6. Satisfaction

You have been understood and the listeners absorbed the content of your presentation like a sponge. They enjoyed your talk and gave you their full attention. You should be proud of yourself because this is a real win-win situation.
Enjoy your success – you have earned it. You want to know what they thought of it and how you can improve things still further? A simple method of doing this is to ask a couple of people for feedback and to enquire specifically as to the strengths and weaknesses of your presentation.

5. Effective presentation in five steps

First things first – anyone can come across as confident. Making a confident impression is something that can also be learnt by those who are shy or have a tendency to speak too fast. The way you come across is to a considerable extent dependant on your own mindset and is a question of practice. Maybe you think this is something reserved for senior management, or for sales or marketing experts. Do you really believe that or do you just want to avoid having to work on learning new skills?
Think about job interviews, heading up meetings, passing on information to designers, developers or the purchasing department, company or product presentations, or the many other occasions when you have to pass on information verbally and therefore have to make some form of presentation. I would like to show you five methods which you can use to help you to come across in a more self-assured way:

1. Change your mindset

You have spent time researching a theme in depth. You are now the greatest expert on this theme! You are the specialist!

2. Vary the way you use your voice

Helga Schäferling, a German social pedagogue, once said, "Sometimes you have to be very quiet in order to be able to hear." Modulate the way you speak. Create tension and gain your listeners' attention by varying the volume and rhythm of your speech. Speak with a higher or a deeper voice to fit in with what you are saying.

3. Make use of gestures and facial expressions

If you want to emphasise certain words, think of appropriate gestures and facial expressions which will underline them. In product presentations, you will often speak about things such as high/low or yesterday/today. Can you think of any gestures which you could use here? What facial expression would you use when you are talking about satisfied customers?

Table 2: Examples of body language

Statement	Body language
Yesterday/today	Indicate to the side with the left/right open hand.
Sales figures are increasing/falling	With your arm bent, move an open hand either upwards or downwards.
All our customers	Both hands form a sphere.
Structured/ systematic	One hand signals beats in steps to the right or left.
Give emphasis	Form a circle with the thumb and index finger. Move the hand so that it counts the beat whilst you say the

4. Maintain eye contact

Maintain eye contact with your listeners so that you can observe their eyes and facial expressions. This means that you will see what they are thinking and will be able to react appropriately with questions or further explanations.

Don't look up at the ceiling, down to the floor or at your toes – you won't find the content of your presentation there. It will also make you look insecure and less credible.

5. Pay attention to your posture

Assume the following position whilst sitting or standing – shoulders back, chest forwards, stomach held in, legs strongly planted on the floor and at shoulder width. How do you feel? Strong and sure of success? That's exactly how others will see you too. Your posture gives away a lot about you, e.g. whether you are sure of yourself or nervous. This can also be perceived when you are sitting down. Depending on what it is you want to achieve, make deliberate changes to your posture. Your posture will also be affected by the clothes you wear. That's why it's important to wear clothes that you feel comfortable in. I'm not talking about your favourite jogging pants, but rather that you dress in a way that is appropriate for the occasion and the target group.

If you are uncertain about what you should wear, then opt for a formal, conservative style of dress. You can't really go wrong with this. There is plenty of information on appropriate dress to be find online. Always remember – first impressions count! You may not get a second chance.

Shortly before the start of your presentation: Walk up to the front with upright posture and head raised – the eyes of the listeners will already be on you and this is your first chance to radiate an air of confidence. Don't stand there as stiff as a soldier, nor as relaxed as if you were meeting up with friends for a beer, and don't walk up and down like a hungry tiger in a cage. Only change your position when you are moving on to a new theme or are introducing a new line of thought.

Are you still feeling unsure as to whether you should change

your style of presentation to make your communication style more effective? Perhaps you are paralysed by the fear of rejection or failure, or of standing out from the crowd.
You need to overcome these fears. Unfortunately, there is no medication which can help you here; the only method is regular practice. Trust me, I have often seen good results with people who were initially insecure and anxious and who were trembling with nerves. As soon as they start applying and internalising these methods, I start to see a completely different person standing there in front of me.

Some good places to practise making a more confident impression:

- in front of the mirror
- when you are playing board games
- when you go out for a walk
- in conversations with strangers/friends
- in any meeting
- at oratory clubs

6. The 'Black box' of your communication

'Black boxes' have been in use for some time now when accidents occur, as a method of analysing a driver's conduct in order to establish the cause of the accident.
You also have a black box where a record of your communication conduct is kept. You are your own black box. It consists of all your much-loved habits of non-verbal communication which you share with those around you.

These silly habits—like frequent clearing of the throat, rubbing your hands together, touching your ear or your nose, pushing your hair behind your ears or standing with your legs crossed— are things which you may not be conscious of yourself. In the field of Communications Psychology, these subconscious communication signals are known as our 'blind spot'.

There are effective ways of getting to know your own blind spot and of getting rid of it:

- Get feedback from your colleagues after presentations, meetings which you have led, talks or workshops.
- Ask someone to film your presentation and then spend some time analysing your behaviour.
- Start by trying to eliminate two silly habits, the ones which are most noticeable. Don't try to get rid of all of them at once.

These 'silly habits' can result in people forming a picture of you as being shy, nervous or incompetent when in fact they are simply habits.

7.   Communication for technical experts

This chapter is devoted to all those of you who are responsible for products who have technical qualifications, work in a company with a technical focus or manage a technical product. You all have something in common – you love technical details and you passionately enjoy telling people about them in great detail. Unfortunately, this interest is not always shared to the same extent by the person you are talking to and your words often bounce off them like water off a duck's back. Your words simply don't get through to them.
Don't take this personally or see it as a lack of interest. It is often the case that your listeners don't understand the technical details, or that the level of detail you are going into is in fact not necessary for them to be able to reach a decision. Here are seven questions for the 'techies' among us – the answers should help you to gauge the appropriate level of technical details to use:

- What precisely is the goal of the information that I am providing?
- What knowledge do I want the participants in the meeting to take away with them when they leave?
- Which decisions are dependent on the information I am providing?
- Are the participants only technical experts or are they rather technical lay persons?
- How can I present my product or analysis findings in such a way that a passer-by on the street, a teenager, or even my grandmother would have a good understanding of what I was saying?
- What types of media, graphics and pictures can I use to support my statements in a simple way?
- What is the maximum amount of time I have available?

Rehearse your presentation in front of a person you know well, so that you can find out if there are any areas that need improving:

- Have sticking points such as frowning, head-shaking or getting distracted ceased to be noticeable in your listener?
- If you are going to be in a large room, can the content of your tables still be read from the back row?
- Can the listener repeat back to you what you have said?
- Does the listener think that all of the content is relevant?

If the answer to any of these questions is 'No', then rework your presentation accordingly. The advantage of good preparation is that you will be sure to achieve the goal you set yourself for your presentation. I can guarantee it!

8.   Understanding the gibberisch of other cultures

"If people are to open a door, they must first know who is standing behind it" (Anke Maggauer-Kirsche)

With these words in mind, I set out into the world as a young manager. In my first career, I travelled throughout Eastern Europe as a garment engineer. I prepared myself mentally for the country and the people in question and learned how to say the most important phrases. Thanks to the internet, the effort involved in this nowadays is considerably less than it was twenty years ago. It's also easy to find lots of fellow human beings from other cultural backgrounds in our own environment who we can ask directly for help. It makes a real difference to the success of your teamwork if the different cultures involved make an effort to meet each other half way. So it was, for example, that the level of quality in one of the manufacturing units rose within one season because I treated the people in charge of production and their employees with respect and showed a genuine interest in what they were doing. The positive flip side of the coin was that they got more enjoyment from their involvement in producing a high-quality product. This is a win-win situation – more enjoyment, better quality, lower costs and less effort for all those involved.
In an interview in the famous newspaper 'Die Zeit', on the theme of 'intercultural competence', Marike Frick once spoke to business coach Gary Thomas, who got straight to the point by saying, "...culture is like a dance – you can't join in if you don't know the steps. And more important, you can't lead. That's why you should always first of all take a look at the others and watch the steps they are taking."
In product management, you will encounter many different cultures, both within the company and externally. You can prevent misunderstandings and conflicts if you first of all familiarise yourself with the other culture. Different cultures can also be an excellent source of inspiration for different points of view, more creativity, tolerance, and a different type

of humour. With the continuing move towards globalisation in our world, intercultural communication skills are a competence which will help you to be more successful in both leadership and in collaboration.

Before we come to a list of tips, I would like to tell you a little cultural anecdote – A Swiss employee had an assignment in Kiel, Germany. After a few meetings, a German colleague of his came up to him and said, "You Swiss are strange people. When you are in agreement, you say 'No, no, that's not a problem.' And when you are against something, then you start with 'Ye-es, but' … How are we supposed to understand you?"

Language skills are of course essential for successful collaboration, but an understanding of different cultures is just as important!

Find out about the key elements of non-verbal and verbal communication in your guest country or in the cultures in the surrounding area. This should help to prepare you for dealing with partners, colleagues and employees in an appropriate way:

- typical phrases for greeting people – written and spoken
- the usual way of saying 'No'
- methods of discussion and negotiation
- small talk themes
- approach towards punctuality
- saying hello and goodbye
- the meaning attached to smiling and gestures
- conduct when it comes to eating and regarding invitations
- dress codes

Show respect towards others and learn to understand their behaviour. This will form a good basis for successful collaboration.

II. COMMUNICATION WITH TEAMS

9. The Open Product Management Workflow™ as a communication booster

by Frank Lemser
The status quo in product management

I often hear from product managers and heads of product management that there is a lot of scope for improvement in the way product management is viewed in their company. They often think that it is only in their company that this is the case. Is this the way you feel too?

At this point, I can offer some reassurance, for experience over the years has shown that the theme of 'lack of respect for product management' is one which is widespread, so you are not alone with your situation.

But why is this the case? Can this situation be improved? Well, here's the good news – you can change the situation at any time. There are several spheres of activity where changes are required in both methods of working and communications in order for product management to receive the high level of respect which it is due.

Open Product Management Workflow™ is a systematic approach which improves communication at all interfaces in such a way that the technical departments, the sales and marketing departments and company management all receive precisely the information that they need for their day-to-day work. By using a style of communication which is tailored to each department, you increase the capacity of the departments to make decisions and reduce the time to market for new products. Fewer suppositions, enquiries and discussions will arise because the information you have supplied is based on real market data.

The causes

1. The language that other people speak is a closed book
Every department in a company has its own specialist and
department-specific language and needs information which has
been amended in line with their language in order for them to
be able to work effectively. Here we can see the cause of the
product manager's basic problem – product managers neither
understand the language of the specialist departments nor do
they have a grasp of the requirements which these
departments have to fulfil. And yet this is the key to success, as
product managers have to collaborate with almost every
department in a company.

*"If there is any one secret of success,
it lies in the ability to get to the other person's point of
view and see things from that person's angle as well as
your own."* (Henry Ford)

Fig. 1: Interfaces where product managers regularly communicate

2. Inappropriate information leads to frustration

Many of the product managers I meet are very focused on technical issues and speak the language of engineers. Marketing and sales staff often tell me how dissatisfied they are with the information they get from product management – "It's always just technical blurb and features which nobody understands". At the product launch, you will find meaningless catchwords on the website and in the brochures and sales materials, such as 'innovative', 'sustainable', 'best' and plenty of technical jargon. The end customers don't understand this either. This kind of thing doesn't help to transform potential customers into buyers and often lengthens the sales process considerably because sales representatives need to engage in a lot more communication in order to convince the customer to purchase the product.

Senior managers report that product management has too little or no knowledge of the market and that the business cases they present do not form an ideal basis when it comes to making decisions on investment in new products. There is a lack of reliable facts based on actual market information as well as of product strategies derived from these which are comprehensible yet also transparent. The arguments presented by product management are simply not convincing enough. As a result, it is often the case that senior management has more faith in their own knowledge and experience than in that of their product managers and has other products developed instead. The result – both sides are frustrated.

The solutions

1. Product managers need to talk to customers

Take a moment to consider what information your management needs in order to be able to make decisions. Can you name the various decisive factors in purchasing as well as the purchasing criteria of your customers?

Are you familiar with the most common problems and needs of the key players in your market?

Do you know the reasons behind the issues that irritate customers, or that cost them time or money, and do you know whether your customers would be prepared to pay out for a good solution?

If you were able to answer all the questions, then you have already done your homework. Experience from actual practice, however, shows that product managers are often unable to provide spontaneous answers to these questions. And yet it is precisely these and further answers that are needed by the senior management, the sales and marketing departments, the technical departments and others besides. And each of them requires the information in a different form.

This is where Open Product Management Workflow™ (www.open-pmw.org) can help you in the systematic passing on of information. Open Product Management Workflow™ starts with the strategic tasks, and the further steps are then derived from these. It provides the right tools for every instance where information is passed on at an interface.

The basis for this workflow is provided by customer interviews to gain information on real problems and needs, as well as further additional customer information. The information from these customer interviews, and thus from the market, give you answers to some important questions, e.g. on the following themes:

- problems with their tasks
- use cases
- user and buyer personalities
- purchasing criteria and purchasing influencing factors
- approach to sourcing information
- situation in regard to competition

These interviews with market players, their evaluation and the specific preparation of the findings for the departments you deal with will form the foundation for your newfound success in communications as a product manager.

In the last six months, how many customer interviews have you held, kept a record of and evaluated?

2. Product managers need to communicate with each department they deal with in a market-focused way

If you want to improve things at the interfaces with other departments and you want to enhance the way that product management is viewed, then ask your internal or external customers what it is that they need in order for them to be more successful, e.g.:

- What are their most common problems?
- What things annoy them or disrupt their work?
- In what areas do they find they are wasting time or money?
- How much would they pay for a solution?

At the very latest after six interviews, the key problem areas will have become clear and you will now have a list of the top problem issues, obtained directly from the market.

Now it's up to you to communicate your findings in a department-friendly way:

Senior management: business plan with real needs, customer segments, sales figures, sales revenue figures, ROI, etc.

Sales and marketing: product positioning, added value, prices, distribution and communication channels, etc.

Product development: prioritised list of requirements in accordance with customer information and company criteria.

Every department receives exactly the information they need to be in a position to make decisions and take action, as they now have actual facts from the market.

It is easy to get real customer information. Nowadays this information is in fact the only important information companies really need to survive in the global market and thus in the competition. If you know what is needed at your interfaces, then you can communicate the market information in a way that suits your customers' needs. By doing so, you cut down on frustration caused by duplicating work, time taken for meetings, wasted investment in development and marketing and, at the same time, you enhance your reputation as a product manager and a competent partner to work with.

10. Gain more with good communication

In almost every training session and every ProductCamp Workshop I lead, I am asked the following question – "How can I find more time to spend on strategic tasks? I get so bogged down with everyday business that I never seem to get round to doing something."
This is for one thing often due to the fact that tasks are not clearly defined and that a product manager is seen as a 'Jack of all trades'. If you feel this is the case for you, then please read chapter nine by Frank Lemser.
Here, however, I would ask you to start with those things which you can have an influence on and can implement, starting tomorrow. The measures in the table to follow have been tested out and work extremely quickly. You can easily save yourself four to ten hours a week by making use of them. You don't believe me? Then make a note of how many e-mails you write over the next three days and how many enquiries you receive asking you for information, amendments or more detailed specifications. How many hours do you spend on these, week by week?

Table 3: Types of communication and potential for improvements

What needs to be done	Your gain in time
E-mails	
Only select the relevant recipients	Avoid receiving floods of e-mails which are not
Content should be goal-oriented and well-structured with clear tasks.	Save time spent on writing and avoid receiving queries.
Consider whether you might get a faster answer via a telephone call.	Cut down on e-mail loops. Discussions go faster on the phone.
Use online tools for surveys.	Avoid floods of e-mails.
Create an appropriate filing system.	Reduce time spent searching for e-mails.
Schedule time in your diary for reading e-	Avoid being disturbed and thus increase productivity.
Text messages/WhatsApp/social media	
Deal with private matters outside of	Focus on one task and thus increase productivity.
Saying no	
Communicate your priorities and offer an alternative	Keep time for the important things and stick to appointments.
Providing information	
Use the language of the recipient. Explain the goal and the background. Give clear information on tasks.	Reduce the number of enquiries which arise due to misunderstandings and lack of information.

11. Facts mean faster decision-making

Business Intelligence systems can provide companies with support in the recording, storage and organisation of data and in making it available in a systematic and precise fashion for the purposes of evaluation. We are well-acquainted with such IT systems in the context of production processes and customer and supplier relationships. Whilst these systems are now in widespread use, we are still waiting for some smart software to be developed that will use customer information to supply the relevant facts for product management.

How are facts currently being dealt with in product management? Let me surprise you with a few facts from a survey I carried out:

- 67% of product managers in managerial roles, 57% of senior product managers and 75% of technical product managers feel that business plans are not based on facts to a sufficient extent.
- 100% of product managers in managerial roles say that innovations are not sufficiently well checked to establish whether they are in line with the needs of the market.
- 60% of product managers in managerial roles and 71% of senior product managers feel that there is room for improvement when it comes to making decisions on the basis of facts.

It is therefore no great surprise to see the findings of the fourth Planview® benchmark study which looked into the challenges faced by product portfolio management:

- In 53% of cases, decisions are unclear, delayed or inefficient.
- Only 15% of those asked have immediate access to up-to-date and precise data.
- 80% of decisions are made on the basis of poor data or data which is difficult to access.

Actinium Consulting came to a shocking result in a study entitled "Those in positions of responsibility in specialist areas are increasingly putting their faith in the analyses of BI systems" – only 33% of those asked feel secure in their decisions, and 40% almost secure.

Looking at these figures, it is easy to understand why decision-making is often delayed. It is high time that new ways were found which would allow product managers to make use of new methods to draw up their proposals for decision-makers on the basis of facts.

Why are facts so important?

As a result of technical complexity, the increase in statutory requirements and the rising demand for products to have user-friendly properties and designs, product development is today much more expensive than it was twenty or thirty years ago. At the same time, the internal expenses of marketing and sales for an international market have also risen. It must therefore be the goal of every company to invest time and money exclusively in developments that really do solve a problem for the customer and provide added value.

"If you aren't solving a problem, then you shouldn't be surprised if nobody is interested in what you are offering." (Peter Sawtschenko)

Market success and the amortisation of expensive developments are the factors that ensure that your company survives and that pay your salary.

Sources for your factual basis

It is not important whether a new solution to a problem comes from customers or from a clever employee. On the other hand, it is of central importance that you examine every idea together with your potential customers and make a record of their statements. You should use the opportunity to collect, update and evaluate data from customers and competitors as well as information on trends. This pool of data provides the foundation for the factual basis which is so often missing in product management. The big advantage of facts is that no hierarchy and no individual person can talk their way around them or deceive anyone with false interpretations. They are real pieces of information obtained from your own scouting activities in the market and not from gazing into a crystal ball!

The list to follow provides you with some useful approaches for collecting general market and customer information:

- User problems, from installation through to disposal
- A need to work more successfully
- Price estimates
- Type of purchasing and type of payment
- Touchpoints before and after the purchase decision
- Information on competitors
- Estimation of business competence

 Now make a note of the things you ask potential customers when you are in conversation. Can you see any potential for improvement for your future interviews?

The more customer interviews you conduct, the more facts you will have at your disposal. With facts that come from customer interviews, you will

- become a competent contact person for senior management and other departments
- make more sustainable decisions
- hold fewer meetings
- facilitate faster and more cost-efficient development
- offer customer-focused products with better margins
- create effective marketing communication
- find the right sales channels

It is still the case that an awful lot of decisions are made every day on the basis of either experience or just gut feeling.

Create some time for yourself to go out into the market. Talk to every kind of customer, competitor and supplier. You will be amazed at the way your market knowledge will grow and how confidently you will be able to sell new ideas internally.

In order that you can experience for yourself the advantages of working with facts as soon as possible, think of a product or product expansion which you will soon be producing a business plan or a catalogue of requirements for. Spend some time determining which facts are missing and try to get hold of these facts. Organise customer interviews to achieve this.

12. Good communications improve motivation

There are diverging opinions on the subject of motivation. Some maintain that people cannot be motivated. Others say that motivating people is most definitely possible.

As a manager I have frequently observed that it is quite clear that people can be motivated, provided they can connect a personal goal with the task in question or are able to understand the significance of the task. I have often established that employees are demotivated because they haven't been given a clear task or have either not been given information on the task in good time or have received no information at all.

You will be justified in arguing that not every task can be considered motivating. You are quite right. However, it is the task of management to explain to employees why any given task is necessary before their level of performance sinks below zero!

When you are assigning tasks, it is important to understand the driving factors which the other person needs to motivate themselves. This driving factor is like the tasty 'carrot' you hold up in front of them. If you have a grasp of this, then it will be easier for you to find arguments in a language which will move the other person to do something for you, for your product, your company or for themselves.

Think about situations when you yourself feel motivated at work:

- when there are new and exciting projects waiting for you?
- when there is the prospect of a sabbatical?
- because of career prospects or the prospect of improving your reputation?
- when you get a pay increase?
- when you are able to work flexibly and in a self-determined way?
- when you will be working with different people?
- when you are sent on regular professional development courses?
- when you get the opportunity to suggest innovative ideas?

Feedback from employees and students has resulted in the following five points which describe the key situations in which people felt motivated in their work:

1. being addressed in person rather than via e-mail
2. clear formulation of tasks
3. information about the necessity and purpose of tasks
4. having trust placed in them to perform well
5. receiving support with questions

It all sounds quite logical, yet projects and teams often fail through the lack of such simple methods of communication. Try in future to be aware that you can have a motivating effect. If you are convinced of the significance of a task, then use a few kind words to explain this, using a clear voice, friendly facial expressions, open gestures and an upright posture. Combine this with some appreciation shown for successes achieved to date or for the personal qualities of the employee in question, and you have already gone a long way towards creating your own unique motivation pills.

13. Improving the level of acceptance of the Product Manager

Enhancing the level of acceptance of a product management department is a Sisyphean task. Clients often tell me how difficult it is to position product management within a company. This is also reflected in the many statements we hear about and from product management – 'Jack of all trades', 'rubbish bin for products and projects nobody wants', "Our product managers just sit at their desks all day", "What do they actually do all day?", "Now I'm going to have product management telling me what to do as well".

In companies with a technical focus, product management has usually already been established, but often works in an insufficiently systematic or customer-focused way and suffers from a poor level of acceptance, not least for this reason, as Frank Lemser also mentions in Chapter 9.
On the one hand, those at the interfaces with sales, development, purchasing, after-sales, testing, marketing and quality management are not well informed about the benefits or the tasks of product management. On the other, they tend to doubt whether product management has the profound knowledge of the market which is required for products to be profitable.

Their colleagues from the technical departments, development, sales or marketing are sometimes even afraid that someone is trying to take away their work or their power. This is because product managers often come into an existing structure and need to find a new position for themselves where they can make use of their knowledge and experience. The other departments first of all wait to see what will be 'delivered'. They have expectations of the product manager, but these have not been expressed. If the product manager doesn't fulfil these expectations, then the other departments will do their job for them. This also applies to the senior management who are hoping to achieve better results, e.g. for business plans, through their micro-management. Yet none of them have told the product manager what their expectations are. Frustration is inevitable, and acceptance remains a long way off.

Why do both those at the interfaces and the senior management have so little faith in product management? Does product management even have confidence in itself? It is as you have already suspected. Trust is something that has to be earned. Creating trust requires work.

"All talk is pointless if there is no basis of trust" (Franz Kafka)

You can increase the level of trust and acceptance for product management in your company to a noticeable extent by employing the following methods:

- Your company, managing director, line manager or HR department issues information internally on the benefits, role and tasks of product management.
- The introduction of product management is carried out as a change management project. It will change the way of thinking and the way things are done in many departments. So, the introduction phase requires time, marketing and sensitivity. It will also mean changes to the tasks of the other departments, and it is important to provide comprehensible information on the benefits and the responsibilities of product management within the company.
- Product managers are given sufficient time to spend in the marketplace. The corresponding travel budget should be planned on an annual basis.
- Product managers are given a platform to carry out their own marketing activities where they can report on experiences, on market and customer knowledge and on successful product launches.

The senior management gives support to product management by providing suitable tools, professional development courses and budgets. Above all, they back product managers when the more traditionally-focused departments prove to be resistant to change.

In this way, the tasks and responsibilities of the product manager become visible, their knowledge of the markets clearly noticeable and product management will be in demand as a competent partner to approach for market knowledge. Do you want to know how long this will take? Until the first occasion when product managers perform convincingly with their market knowledge – with the first business plan, with the drawing up of a requirements specification or with product positioning.

 What measures are suitable to increase the level of trust for your department? Write them down as action items for you.

14. Performance indicators for Product Manages

The value of product management for a company is significantly underestimated. We often hear statements such as "Product managers only produce paper and are not productive", "You can't measure what they achieve", "I only ever see product managers producing PowerPoint presentations". Every company that has product management is pursuing the goal of a profitable product portfolio. How can they succeed in presenting the true worth of product management?

A proven method of making achievements visible is the use of performance indicators. (PI) We are familiar with their use in other departments, e.g. in production, sales or logistics. Why are there not yet any PI for the achievements of product management widely used?

Here too, PI can highlight strengths and weaknesses and lead to a more targeted fostering of the 'product manager as a market expert'. It is therefore important that we use performance indicators that can only be influenced by the product manager. For this reason I am not proposing the use of the usual product performance indicators, such as margin, turnover, etc.

Table 4: Performance indicators (PI) to measure the achievements of a product manager

PI	Content	Possible effects
Market expertise	Time in the market related to overall working hours. Number of customer interviews conducted per month.	Improved knowledge of customers and markets, customer-focused products, higher product margins. Gain access to facts on the market, fewer errors in investment.
Time-to-market	Time from the idea through to the creation of a business plan, number of meetings for coordination with the development department.	Faster time-to-market, competitive advantage, higher sales revenue at an earlier stage.
Portfolio profitability	Stock turnover per product, number of support enquiries, number of guarantee	Less capital tied up, timely product elimination, increase in liquidity, freeing up of employee resources
Customer satisfaction	Satisfaction with product trainings, profitability	Recommendations, higher sales figures, faster amortisation

These PIs help to make the benefit and value provided by the product manager more visible for both senior management and those at the interfaces. They also serve as a way of controlling and optimising the performance of product managers.

15. How does Generation Y tick?

The term digital natives refers to all those young people who were born after 1981 and have grown up with digital media. This generation gets more attention than Generation X as they have grown up with a different technical culture. Generation X comprises all those individuals who were born between 1960 and 1980. It is also the generation who have grown up with a stable economy and without there being any material shortages in the Western world. It is therefore not surprising that existential needs hardly play a role in Generation Y academic circles. In a study by Wagner entitled 'Beware of stereotypes – what motivates Generation Y', it was established that Generation Y is much more heterogeneous that had previously been supposed.

Sometimes I get the feeling that Generation Y is a just a product of the media. I do remember all the things that have been said about the 1980s generation – "Can't be bothered generation", "Stupid from too much TV", "They are only interested in consuming", "They are only interested in money". This gives me a feeling of déjà vu and I believe it is in fact a sign of fear in dealing with new kinds of personalities.

The first Generation Y product managers are now well into their professional careers and have been for some years. We can no longer entice Generation Y managers with the 'old trappings of power' such as high salaries and bonuses. These 20 to 30-year-olds are changing the remuneration market. According to a 2014 study by Diehl, entitled 'Clichés about Generation Y don't come anywhere near the reality', involving 1,000 young academics in Germany, it was established that the most common needs and values were as follows:

- self-determination
- security
- good working atmosphere
- being appreciated

- change
- mobility
- trust
- autonomy
- feeling at ease

All the studies I have read on this theme were conducted with academics or prospective academics. My own Generation Y students, who are all employed in production, tell me that salary is in fact most definitely right at the top of their list.

If you find yourself in the position of having to confront the values of Generation Y because you want to take on a young product manager or you are trying to mediate in a situation of conflict, then I would like to offer you a list of the top seven motivational factors for Generation Y, according to Wagner:

1. Enjoyment of the work
2. Professional development
3. A sense of purpose to the work
4. Monetary remuneration
5. Career opportunities
6. Work-life balance
7. Location

Get used to providing individual employment packages and ask the individuals in question what their personal wishes are. Keep in mind the following tips in your everyday dealings with members of Generation Y:

- Give clear briefs, but with freedom in the way they deal with their work
- Show particular appreciation for performance
- Allow flexibility in working hours and environment
- Create a good working atmosphere with open lines of communication
- Trust them to do their work

16. Meetings which are more beneficial for everyone

The survey 'Communication in Product Management' shows that meetings are the most common form of communication for product managers in managerial roles and senior product managers. Their level of satisfaction with this form of communication, however, is below 50%. This gives food for thought, as 64% of those questioned said that they themselves were very successful when it came to running meetings. 67% of product managers with a technical focus said they would be interested in receiving training in the running of meetings. However we look at it, the fact remains that the 20 to 30 hours per week which product managers spend in meetings are not always being put to good use.

"A meeting is an event which involves many people going in and not much coming out" (Werner Fitz)

In this chapter, you will be provided with a tool kit which you can use to bring your meetings to a close on time and to achieve the goals you have set yourself as the person chairing the meeting.

1. Always prepare an agenda. Even when you need to hold a meeting at very short notice, take a moment to think about the content, the order and the key results you want to achieve from the meeting and write these down on a piece of paper or a flip chart before starting. Usually, an agenda will indicate the themes to be discussed, decisions that need to be made, who is responsible for what and the time frame for the points of discussion. A meeting may last 15 or 20 minutes. You don't need to set aside 60 minutes just because this happens to be the custom. Take as much time as is necessary but no more than this.
2. Inform the other contributors well in advance about the time frame and content of the meeting, and the goal of the information being provided.
3. Gather information beforehand on the characters of those

taking part and give some thought to how you plan to deal with people who talk too much, powerful decision-makers, shy individuals or strong Alpha types. If you are looking for new ideas or need to get an estimation of budgets, for example, and you have both shy characters and their line managers in the meeting, then consider using anonymous voting methods or other creative solutions.

4. When it comes to those who simply talk too much, you may and should interrupt them in a friendly way. You could, for example, say, "Mr Allgood, many thanks for your explanation but would you mind getting to the point? We will be moving on to the next point in three minutes' time." Another possible approach would be to say "I can see that you still need further information or clarification. We can deal with this after the meeting, just the two of us. Let's move on now to point 3."

5. Send out documentation regarding decisions to be made or presentations, in the ideal case at least four days before the meeting, so that the participants have time to get prepared.

6. Avoid unrest or disruption caused by poor conditions in the room or unsuitable infrastructure by checking the room in advance and making any necessary changes.

7. Start the meeting by greeting all the participants in a friendly manner. Go through the content of the documents you sent out to them, as not everyone will have read them.

8. Agree on rules for your meetings, e.g. if people are not properly prepared, then the meeting should be cancelled. Attendees who regularly turn up late should pay an agreed sum into a kitty. Mobile phones should be switched off or at least not allowed on the table. Rules such as these can be decisive in achieving a calm and quiet atmosphere and in keeping to the time allotted.

9. Close the meeting by thanking the attendees for their time and their participation, summarise the key decisions

and outstanding points and state when you will be sending out the minutes. Be sure to type up the minutes or at least a note and let them know when these will be sent out and where the document will be filed. Drawing up minutes can save time and even save your neck, when a colleague comes up to you later and asks, "Where will I find …?"

10. Despite all your preparation and best efforts to run the meeting well, it may still be the case that you underestimated the time required or that new information has come to light, meaning that there are still points outstanding at the end of the meeting. First of all, ask the participants whether you can extend the meeting. If this is not possible, then arrange another meeting for the outstanding points to be dealt with and close the meeting in accordance with point 9.

These points may sound simple and indeed they are. The secret to success lies in consistent application of the rules and in having the courage to leave behind your old ways and try something new. If it isn't usual to write minutes in your company, then introduce the practice. You don't have an agenda? Then draw one up and send it out via e-mail and demonstrate to the participants the advantage of this change in procedure. In my experience, everyone is happy if meetings achieve results and use up less time.
If you are not in fact chairing the meeting and you have attended yet another unsatisfactory meeting, then ask the person running the meeting whether they would mind if you gave them some feedback.

Take a Post-it and write down the points from the list above which you could use to improve your own meetings. Stick it on your PC in a visible location or set yourself a task related to this in your diary. Try to implement the improvements in the next meeting you hold.

17. Talking to 'difficult' employees

In the survey 'Communication in Product Management' which looked at the most common types of communication, 'Communication with difficult team members' was listed in fourth place in the various weekly tasks mentioned. 55.6% of the respondents were product managers with managerial roles or senior product managers. But how can we define 'difficult team members'? Employees who have been with the company for many years and have tunnel vision? Members of the team who often turn up late? A Generation Y employee who has different needs to yours in terms of working environment? Generally speaking, we perceive employees to be 'difficult' if they

- do not complete their assigned tasks
- do not perform well
- refuse to do tasks or refuse to communicate
- are highly motivated yet do not perform well
- are lacking in social skills

Communication with difficult members of the team can sometimes feel like climbing the Himalayas – hard work and you don't know whether you will reach the summit. Yet it is possible to learn how to get to the top. You just need the right equipment!
I am now going to describe four techniques which will help to avoid frustration on both sides. You will then once again be able to create a positive and motivating team atmosphere which will make it is easy and enjoyable for everyone to get on with their work.

1. Give them attention
Analyse the situation by taking a look at the point of view of the team member in question. Ask targeted questions to establish what is bothering or hindering them and find out what their personal goals are. Listen attentively. This is an ability that is slipping further and further into the background in today's high-

speed digital world. And yet giving people attention, showing interest in their affairs and taking time to talk to them often prove to be the key to success.

2. Communicate clearly

In my conversations with product managers, I frequently hear tales of them being given assignments which they don't understand. They interpret them as best they can and make a guess as to what was intended, then full steam ahead, but often they are heading for disaster. What a waste of time and energy! The consequences are unavoidable – if the results are poor, then the product manager and this line manager are both frustrated and there is talk of 'incompetence'. I would therefore recommend that you take the time to formulate tasks as precisely as possible and try to be transparent when it comes to the background of the task. And be sure to ask your team member whether they have properly understood the task.

3. Give constructive feedback

One of the most important social skills of a manager is the ability to give feedback. Spending some time giving feedback to the 'difficult' team member regarding their behaviour or performance is one of the most effective and easiest means of aiding their personal development.

Unfortunately, I hear all too often in training sessions that praise is still rarely given. Thinking 'not being reprimanded should be considered praise enough' is just not true! Recognition is like a mother's milk to her baby – it strengthens our defence systems and helps us to develop as individuals. Many people find it difficult to tell others when their behaviour or performance at work is not to their personal liking. We are often afraid of offending or hurting them because we have never learned the right way to give feedback. Giving feedback does not mean saying "There are lots of mistakes in this. Please rework it." No-one likes hearing this kind of criticism.

Feedback that helps a person develop is built from the following building blocks:

1. Always start with a positive statement.
2. Describe the inadequate performance or the undesirable behaviour in specific terms. Use an example and avoid being condescending.
3. Explain the effect this had on you. When doing this, speak in the first person.
4. Keep the focus on the positives for improvements.
5. End the conversation with a friendly and motivating closing comment, which suggests to the other person that you mean well.

The example above could be used as follows for a feedback session:
"Many thanks for sending me the assignment on time. I noticed that there were a few inadvertent mistakes in the business plan and some of the graphics were illegible. This made it difficult for me to read the text quickly and to understand it. Could you go through it again and have it back to me tomorrow? Otherwise it looks great."
Admittedly the second version is going to take a little longer. However, the employee wasn't reprimanded and was not judged, but was instead shown appreciation and knows exactly what needs to be done now. That should be worth two minutes of your time.

4. Involve the team member in the search for a solution

As a rule, most of the people we deal with are healthy adults who want to take responsibility for their own actions. So ask the team member in question what they think the best solution would be and what contribution they could make to improving things. If you are lucky, this solution will be exactly in line with your own ideas, plus one big advantage – the employee proposed the solution themselves and will feel responsible for putting it into practice. It is not a solution 'that has come from above'.
When you realise that things have become more relaxed again in the team, opinions are being openly expressed and your

colleagues are once again treating one another with respect, then you have succeeding in doing your job as a manager. You, the team member in question and the rest of the team will all be pleased to see that a good atmosphere and good performance have been restored.

18. Recognising 'difficult' employees

In the previous chapter, you have learned how to deal with difficult employees and team members. Yet how do we define a 'difficult' employee? We all have personality traits that can be perceived as being 'difficult', depending on the environment we are in. People may be seen by the team as being difficult if they block communication or perhaps lead the discussion in the wrong direction, or if they question things or are too loud. The definition of a 'difficult' team member or employee is very much dependent on the perception of the viewer and their own personality type.

In the following section, I would nevertheless like to highlight some personality types which are typically considered to be 'difficult'. Should you encounter such individuals, then you will have some possible courses of action at your fingertips to enable you to restore a harmonious working atmosphere.

Table 5: Behaviour and ways of dealing with difficult stereotypes

Type	Behaviour	How to deal with it
Moaner	Puts problems and difficulties in the foreground.	Give constructive feedback. Involve the 'moaner' in finding solutions and give them responsibility for this.
Narcissist	Very self-assured, sometimes comes across as arrogant, everything revolves around them.	Give constructive feedback on their behaviour. Ask other employees to tell their success stories. Delegate tasks to the narcissistic individual which require them to give recognition to the achievements of others.
Little helper	Friendly and socially-minded. They can't say no and don't manage to complete their own work.	Give them priorities and set time limits which you should then monitor. Explain to them the effect it has when we try to help everyone.
Depressed	Pessimism is the order of the day. The world is a bad place, nothing ever works out and they don't enjoy many	Take time to talk and find out the reasons behind this attitude. Come to agreements on how motivation can be increased, and things can be made more enjoyable. Include the team
Challenging	Recognition is important. Critical about the achievements of others, often in a bad mood for no apparent reason.	Try to use empathy as this type of person is very insecure and is looking for confirmation from others. Give them challenging tasks and projects which they can use to boost their profile.

19. Conflict Management – The calm after the storm

As a manager, you may have the option of choosing your product managers through the recruitment process, but you don't have any choice when it comes to your superiors or your colleagues at the wide range of interfaces which you deal with. In contrast to our private lives, at work we cannot select our partners and it is expected of us that we get on well with others. And, as the world of work is filled with all sorts of colourful and interesting personalities, with a wide range of needs and requirements, conflicts will inevitably arise every now and then. This is normal like a storm. It heralds its arrival and then, after a lot of noise and bluster, the air is cleared. It's a good idea to see conflict in this way.

You will have noticed that I have mentioned conflicts here which arise on account of problems in interpersonal relations. Conflicts may of course also arise due to the type or number of tasks assigned, or because of organisational changes, etc. Yet most conflicts which I have experienced or been involved with are of an interpersonal nature.

The most important thing in a situation of conflict is to recognise that it exists and to solve it quickly. Politely looking the other way is rarely a good solution; after all, you don't want a little smouldering fire to develop into a full-scale blaze. Don't try to deny that there is a conflict or avoid the issue – if you ignore it, it will come back at you like a boomerang, in the form of low performance, a bad atmosphere, absenteeism or even with someone handing in their notice.

"When someone stops speaking to you, it means they want to say something to you" (Joachim Panten)

Be brave and address conflicts openly. Take a systematic approach by setting up a conversation aimed at resolving the conflict. I say conversation here because this type of communication should not be carried out via e-mail. After such a conflict resolution session, you will usually find that you and the employee or colleague in question can once again look one another in the eye in a relaxed manner.

You will both be pleased and thankful for this positive development in the situation.

How to recognise potential conflicts:
- a person repeatedly remaining silent
- frequent absence from meetings
- absence due to sickness
- a mood of resignation
- more formal behaviour or being overly polite
- gossiping and/or spreading rumours
- aggressive behaviour
- opinionated behaviour and/or frequent contradiction of others
- playing down problems

Six key questions to help you prepare yourself for a conflict resolution session:
1. What issues have led to the conflict?
2. What is the current situation?
3. What is the relationship basis?
4. How do you feel at the moment?
5. What aspects are not acceptable?
6. What changes are you hoping to achieve?

For a successful conflict resolution session:
- Choose the right time, not Monday morning or Friday late afternoon.
- Get well-prepared in advance.
- Listen carefully to what the other person has to say.
- Show respect and don't bring emotions into the equation.
- Stay focused on the future and on solutions.
- Limit the time for the meeting to 20 to 30 minutes.

 Do you have any experience of conflict resolution sessions? How did you feel? Reflect on which aspects of the conversation were positive and which were not so good, and then read on.

Table 6: Conflict resolution sessions in five steps

Step	Content	Description
Step 1	Your concern	Explain your own goals and wishes in a transparent and comprehensible way and if appropriate demonstrate your willingness to change. Point to the possible consequences if a change in the situation is not achieved.
Step 2	Your goal	Listen attentively to what the other person has to say and take note of their behaviour when they are doing so. Don't make any judgement of what they say. Clarify any aspects which are not clear to you and ask them for suggestions for a solution.
Step 3	Find mutualities	Which common goals are you both pursuing for the company, the department or the project?
Step 4	Look for solutions	Find and discuss possible solutions which would be in line with the needs and wishes of both parties. Don't be persuaded into any "poor compromises" as this would mean that the conflict had not actually been solved.
Step 5	Agree on a plan of action	Write down the solution and the way it is to be implemented, with a defined deadline. On this date, you can celebrate together, or otherwise bring in a mediator if an improvement has not been achieved.

III. CUSTOMER-FOCUSED COMMUNICATION
20. Listening increases the amount of information acquired

"Ms Laubner, could you repeat that please? I didn't quite catch what you said." It is after all difficult—at least it would be for me—to send out jokes on WhatsApp and listen to a product briefing at the same time. If your internal and external customers don't listen attentively, then valuable time is wasted in repeating the information. And if you are quite honest, it is pretty annoying too.

As a product manager, you will often find yourself in the role of the listener. You are invited to a lot of meetings and you have conversations with your customers. If you are a good listener, then you can repeat back the content of what has been said, and you can give appropriate answers or ask further questions on the theme. This requires you to devote yourself entirely to the speaker and to listening to what they are saying. It doesn't mean that you simply hear what is said, or that you only listen to the extent that you are aware that something is being said. It means that you are absorbing what is being communicated to you with every single nerve cell in your body. In the ideal case, you will also make it clear to the speaker whilst you are listening that right now the only thing you are interested in is their information.
Here are some tips for successful listening:

- Show through your posture that you are giving the speaker your full attention.
- Use your facial expressions and gestures to show that you are open to what they are saying.
- Don't interrupt the other person – let them finish their sentences.

- Be aware of the messages that body language, facial expressions and gestures convey.
- Give confirmation every now and then that you are listening, with a nod or a "Yes" or "I see", or with a question, such as "Could you explain that in a bit more detail?"
- Make notes.
- Turn off all forms of digital media.
- Put your phone somewhere out of your sight.
- Ask questions if things are not clear.

As a product manager, if you develop the ability to listen actively then you will get positive feedback from customers, partners and colleagues, as well as a lot of valuable information as input for new products or for improvements to existing products.

Improve your ability to give someone your full attention by selecting a maximum of three of the above-mentioned points which you could use to make an immediate improvement in your own behaviour.

21. Product Managers gain knowledge of the markets

In my training courses for product managers who want to gain certification, customer interviews are cited as the key source of information for the facts which are used in business plans, catalogues of requirements and marketing communications. These customer interviews are, however, not organised by the sales department but rather by the product manager. As a representative of the market, the product manager, together with his/her team, is responsible for creating the right products, and therefore needs to have first-hand knowledge.

Yet the conversations I have had indicate that product managers often don't take the time—or are not given authorisation—to find out what is going on in the market.

The training to become a certified product manager therefore also includes training in conducting such customer interviews.

This allows some first experience to be gained in a safe environment. Most product managers say that they immediately start to think of solutions and communicate these to the customer. They also frequently realise that they are no longer following up to find out exactly what the customer has said – they haven't been focusing
on what the customer is saying. This wouldn't be possible anyway when the brain is programmed to search for solutions. Fortunately, all the participants recognise that use of the key question words can be practised (who, what, when, where, why, how) so they can lead the conversation in such a way as to gain a good deal of information from it.

"There is nothing you can't get if you ask in the right way!"
(Ivor Spencer, International School for Butlers)

The decisive factors in customer interviews:
1. Set yourself a goal for the interview and a time frame.
2. Inform the customer of the purpose and the date/time of the meeting.
3. Take with you the questions you have prepared.
4. Be careful not to go through your questions by ticking them off like a checklist, as this will stop the flow of conversation and may irritate the customer.
5. Use question words (who, what, when, where, why, how) – How do you use our products? What problems have arisen in use? What features could be added to improve the product and save you time or money? Why did you opt for the competitor's product? If money was not an issue, what would your ideal solution be? Why is it that you can't achieve the required number of units with our product?
6. Ask the customer to describe some typical use cases.
7. Listen attentively and follow up with further questions if the customer provides new information which points to new problem areas or shortcomings.
8. If appropriate, ask further questions if there is something you haven't understood.

9. Avoid suggestive questions, i.e. making a claim but formulating it as a question, e.g. "Surely you think that the new RFID technology is the best solution for this problem?"

Avoid trying to influence the customer's opinion in any way during the conversation.

A further obstacle which product managers often bring up is the sales department. Sales has a lot of power, especially when it comes to products which require a lot of explanation. They don't want to give away 'their' customer data and they don't want the product managers going to 'their' customers on their own.

This hurdle too can be elegantly crossed if you highlight the potential benefits to the sales staff:

- You are not checking up on their work but rather trying to find out how well the product's performance and the marketing and sales material are understood by the customer.
- You want to get an understanding of the customer and his needs in order to create products which are easier to sell.
- You want to find out whether further products might still be needed and what kind of products they might be so that you can enable the company to manufacture a profitable range of products.

If they still refuse to allow you to go 'on your own', then ask them to come along to the first few meetings. I have yet to meet a sales employee who would turn down this offer. What I have often experienced, however, are sales staff who are amazed at how much customers have to say when nothing is being sold to them.

Information on customers' wishes and on user problems is not only to be found in interviews on the customers' premises, however, but also at trade shows, training sessions, experience groups or round tables. Support enquiries, satisfaction surveys, quality reports and warranty ratings will also provide you with information which comes directly from the customer. In this way, you will build up the knowledge of the market which is expected of you.

Take some time to discuss your new approach with a sales colleague who is open to new ideas or favourably disposed towards you and practise your line of argument. Make sure you also inform your line manager so that no one is surprised at what you are doing.

22. Precise customer requirements reduce costs

In training sessions on the Open Product Management Workflow™, product managers are asked to draw up a specification for a particular product. 90% of them formulate their customer needs along the following lines:

- lighter in weight
- user-friendly
- modern
- sustainable

These are the kind of requirements which development or purchasing departments receive on a daily basis. Now put yourself in the shoes of the developer or the purchasing manager. You will soon find yourself coming up with questions – "What does lighter in weight mean? What needs to be more user-friendly? What does 'modern' mean for us?"
This is exactly how the poor developers and purchasing managers feel. It's not only product managers who you need to feel sorry for when they are expected to have yet another new idea up their sleeve without really having understood the problems of the customer or the marketplace. Developers too find that customer requirements like these don't bring them any enlightenment, but rather leave them still fumbling around in the dark.

The escalation pyramid which arises through such a diffuse set of requirements is as follows:

- The developer doesn't start work on a solution.
- You receive an invitation to a further meeting for clarification.
- The developer designs the functionality to the best of his knowledge and abilities, and according to his own experience.
- Countless samples are produced, none of which is ultimately used.
- There are several meetings to discuss customer benefits.
- It isn't possible to produce targeted marketing communications.
- Customers don't understand the product and don't buy it.
- Company profits are down, and jobs are endangered.

The 'do it right the first time' principle also applies to the processes in product management. When you get an order, simply handing over a rapidly drawn-up set of specifications so that the work package can be ticked off means that you are not just jumping from the frying pan into the fire; you are in fact heading for disaster.

The provision of precisely formulated information and assignments is a key factor in goal-driven work processes with a minimum of effort in both the technical departments and in production and logistics. After all, when you order something for your personal needs, you would hardly forget to supply your name and full address, complete with house number and post code!

From now onwards, provide more specific definitions of what you mean by a lighter weight, or by user-friendly or modern. For example:

Lighter in weight = make reference to the predecessor product, the competitor's product or another object with a specific weight.

<u>User-friendly</u> = just one click to the purchase process, or an audible signal when the machine has a fault; a 50% increase in the font size.

Through customer interviews or observational studies, you can find out when, where and how often the problems arise. You can describe these in a user scenario, for example:
"Max would like to use his e-bike to go to work each morning. As he keeps his bike in the cellar, he has to carry it up the stairs every morning. He has problems lifting the bike, which weighs 50 pounds, and has already got marks on his clothes several times in the process. The rechargeable battery weighs 12 pounds and can be taken out, but this would mean going up and down the stairs twice and would use up too much time. Max would like to have an e-bike that doesn't weigh more than 20 pounds including the battery."
With this information, the resourceful developer can start to look for an appropriate solution for their customer 'Max'.
And even better:
The testing department are now able to define quality criteria and testing procedures on the basis of the description. They can devise tests to establish whether the developers have solved the customer's problem.
The documentation of precise customer requirements takes time. For this reason, it is to be recommended that you try to achieve a good level of standardisation so that you are not constantly reinventing the wheel. For example, standardisation is possible for internal guidelines, for ISO (International Electrotechnical Commission) or IEC (International Organisation for Standardisation) standards or legal bases.

Now, here is an important task for you. Take a current set of specifications, a product specification or the nearest business plan to hand. Go through it and mark all the areas where you feel that facts or precise information are missing. What improvements for your own work can you derive from this?

23. Prioritising customer requirements

How do customer and market requirements make their way into the new product? Books on product management rarely tell us how product requirements should be described and evaluated. How are technical product managers or product owners supposed to know how to proceed?

In the 2014 Swiss Product Management Study, it was established that those companies who recorded growth for sales revenue and profit in double figures, as well as a continuous expansion of market share, were all companies who consider an understanding of customer needs and customer behaviour to be the key factor in their success.

In many meetings, however, product requirements are mostly defined according to the following criteria:

- An important trading partner requires this function.
- The sales department say they can't sell the product without this function.
- The competition has it too.
- The function is 'state-of-the-art'.
- "I know what our customers want."
- Studies have shown that …
- In my experience, we need …

Did you notice anything in particular? None of them stated that a number of customers have a common problem and that the new solution will make a contribution towards solving it. The fact is, however, that neither the sales department nor the trading partners will be able to sell anything if the customer doesn't need it.

The dream sales era is over – the times when customers with sparkling eyes would snap up every new product on the market. Customers in the B2B and B2C environment are better informed than ever and carry out their own in-depth research, both online and offline. This means that companies who want to be successful need to develop products which fulfil customer expectations. If the new function doesn't solve any problems for the customer and doesn't bring them any relevant improvement in their situation, then valuable man hours and company funds are simply being thrown out of the window.

I would like to give you a few arguments to explain why it makes no economic sense to initiate a new product idea or product improvement solely at the wish of an individual sales representative,

unless you are working in the project business and are fulfilling customer orders.

Why it doesn't make sense for a company to fulfil the wishes of an individual customer:

- The development team will be burdened with unplanned tasks.
- The new product will prevent deadlines from being met for the delivery of other product development work.
- The product will require comprehensive documentation.
- The new product will have to be dealt with in development, sales, after-sales, ERP, and quality and release management.
- Warehousing costs and purchasing costs may rise.
- Product management will need to deal with the administration for the additional products.
- The customer is not prepared to pay the costs across the entire life cycle of the product.

You can see here that this whim of the sales department will have far-reaching consequences. It is therefore your task to test out the market to see whether this problem in fact exists for several customers. If it will indeed be worth the company investing in the solution of the problem, then draw up a business plan and proceed strategically so that the right product is developed. The product's features can then be planned according to the product strategy which has been set out.

One participant in a training session recently said to me, "This 'feature fucking' is driving me crazy. It doesn't solve the real problems of our customers." This is a statement which I often hear in one form or another. Without knowledge of the customer, you will simply be pouring money down the drain with countless meetings with discussions on assumptions of what the customer wants. This leads to wasted time on account of delays in decision-making and unnecessary designs, samples and prototypes.

A better approach is the one taken by Pilatus Aircraft Ltd in Stans (Switzerland). Many years ago, they started asking customers of the jet PC-12 where they were currently experiencing problems, where they saw the challenges of the future and what their vision was for the aircraft of the future. By doing this, they found out that longer distances needed to be covered in a shorter time and, above all, that jet aircraft needed to be able to land on shorter runways and to be able to carry both passengers and freight. In 2015, their first jet aircraft, with a length of 17 metres, flew across Central Switzerland and was thus presented to a broad section of the public. Within two days, they had orders for 84 jet aircraft at a unit price of 8.9 million dollars.

How did this traditional propeller plane manufacturer manage to arouse the interest of so many customers?

If you want to make products that solve real customer problems and bring genuine added value, there is only one solution:

As the person responsible for the product, you need to have market knowledge.

You can use the information from customer interviews in your communications with the development department – in the form of a prioritised catalogue of requirements.

Before providing you with a formula for prioritisation to make your everyday life much easier, you'll see a list the criteria which are typically used to prioritise product requirements:

- Gut feeling
- "The boss told me to do it like that"

- Estimations of the amount of work and of costs
- Potential earnings
- Urgency on account of support enquiries
- Whoever shouts the loudest

I bet you had a smile at the beginning of the list, then a nod and, with the last one, wondered who that might be. Have no doubt, this is how priorities are actually set in many companies. Here is the solution:

Together with your senior management, define criteria for the importance of a development, e.g.:

Legal requirements = weighting of 99
Decisive buying criterion for evaluating customers = 3
Potential customer is losing time, money, image = 2
Existing customer cannot reach his targets = 1
Nice to have = 0

Multiply the figures for these criteria by the answers gained from customer interviews and you will arrive at a priority list with real customer focus.

Table 7: Prioritised list of requirements according to Open Product Management Workflow™

Requirements (market problem solved)	Importance	Frequency	Priority
Fewer CO_2 emissions	99	5	495
Realtime stop via text message	3	20	60
Wi-Fi access	2	30	60
Support 24/7	2	25	50
Large screen	1	15	15

This market-based function/frequency table is ideal for setting priorities in a transparent way and for getting rid of the typical evaluation procedure often used by the development department.

Many senior managers want to integrate additional company-specific criteria in this evaluation scheme, such as costs, expense of development, innovation, etc. These can be taken into account in the formula for setting priorities.
Assuming you receive a request to extend this list for a B2B product
to include the criteria 'Innovation' (I) and 'Development costs' (D), then assign each of the additional criteria one point. The priority list would then be calculated as follows:
Importance x Frequency x (1+I+D) = priority

Table 8: Prioritising an extended list of requirements

Requirements (market problem	Importance	Frequency	I	D	Priority
Fewer CO2 emissions	99	5		1	990
Wi-Fi access	2	30	1	1	180
Realtime stop via text message	3	20	1		120
Support 24/7	2	25			50
Large screen	1	15	1		30

This priority list is easily understood and shows at a glance the market problems which the developer needs to focus on.
Discuss this approach with your line manager and with the head of the development department and highlight the advantages.
Set up a meeting to present the new method and to carry out a

brainstorming session for 'entrepreneurial' criteria.

What should you do if the method is rejected? Work according to the simple prioritisation demonstrated in Table 8. The benefits which come from the use of this prioritised list of requirements will make your work much easier as well as considerably simplifying the work of those you deal with at the interfaces.

24. "Let me have a look" – Visualisation for better products

by Katharina Brunner

I'm sure you all have experience of those ad hoc project meetings called at short notice? And of working through the night in the closing phase of product development? And of endless requests for changes from a diverse array of stakeholders? A good way of preventing this kind of stress is to make sure that your communication is tailored to the recipient, goal-driven and arrives in good time. For you as a product manager, the most important thing is that there is a common understanding of the future product.

Prototyping supports this common understanding in a product development team in a better way than any other method. At any phase of the development work, visualising a product helps all those involved to find a common basis and ensures that they are all speaking the same language. A prototype ensures that any personal interpretations and suppositions are taken out of the picture. This means that unnecessary discussion is avoided, as are erroneous steps in development which are costly and a waste of valuable time.

Four reasons for visualisation by means of prototypes

Is prototyping not yet well established in your company? Here are four arguments in favour of visualising your product:

1. Joint efforts at visualisation or prototype discussions promote collaboration in the team. Documentation and specifications can be interpreted in various different ways but a prototype is something tangible.

2. By using a prototype, it is easy to make an assessment as to whether particular features or design elements would be feasible or make sense. This is done *before* anything has actually been manufactured.

3. Presenting a prototype is a great method of selling an idea and of persuading sceptical stakeholders to come on board.

4. A prototype can be tested out on end customers early on in the development process. This allows problems regarding user-friendliness to be picked up on and eliminated, prior to actual delivery of the product.

From rough to refined

Visualisation is a process which involves a number of stages of refinement. It starts with rough sketches and extends via detailed wireframes and mock-ups through to a complex and refined prototype.

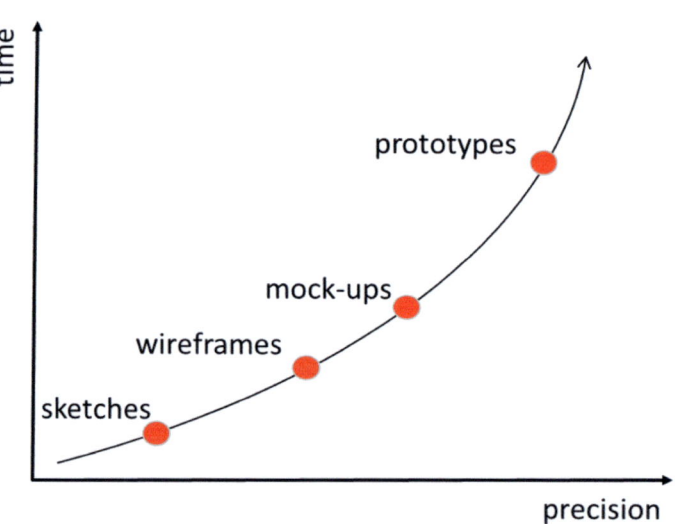

Too much precision in the initial stages of a product's development is a waste of time and money. The magic word here is iteration:

The first designs and new features are presented by means of simple sketches. Over the course of several versions, these sketches become increasingly detailed.

Sketches

Simple sketches are well-suited for use in customer interviews and for innovations. Sketches can be done anywhere and everywhere. All you need is a pen and paper, a blackboard or white board, a tablet or even the proverbial serviette or beer mat. Save these sketches by taking a photo, as there may come a time when they are needed again.

Wireframes

Wireframes, CAD models or renderings are the next stage, with an increased level of precision. They are used to give an approximate depiction of structures and content. But still without any detail in terms of function. Wireframes can be developed by hand on paper or drawn up with the help of suitable software.

Mock-ups

Mock-ups are models or imitations of the future product. They demonstrate the visual design, but still without any interactivity. They are usually created with a prototyping tool and are often used for A/B testing.

Prototypes

Prototypes display the highest level of precision. They depict the functionality of the future product and are highly suitable for usability tests. They can be used for actual 'proof of concept'. They represent the most important means of communication within the entire development team and with customers.

There is in the meantime a wide range of different programmes for the visualisation of products and new ones seem to appear on an almost weekly basis. In the list below, you will find a selection of tools which have proven their worth:

Table 9: Software tools for prototyping (a selection)

Software	Advantages	Disadvantages
Presentation software (PowerPoint, Keynote, etc.)	in very widespread use and easy to use	limited when it comes to collaboration and interactivity
Keynotopia	collection of design templates for PowerPoint or Keynote for a diverse range of operating systems	no interactivity
Graphic software (Photoshop, Sketch, etc.)	in widespread use	requires a lot of expertise, often too detailed
Prototyping (wireframes, mock-ups) • Balsamiq • Mock-ups • MockFlow WireframePro	easy to use, many libraries (templates), export and presentation options	limited interactivity
Prototyping (prototypes) • Axure RP • UXPin • InVision • Proto.io	many templates, often with collaboration functions, enables interactivity	complex functionality, time-consuming learning process

As a product manager, you mustn't allow yourself to get confused or led astray. The project plan for each product will need to include several prototyping steps as milestones, and you can use these visualisations to discuss the product with your team and your stakeholders. The cost of a design mock-up or a prototype can easily run into four figures.

Yet how much do four or five meetings cost, with eight team members present in each case?

And what about the costs of delays and the development of the wrong functions or design elements? By using prototypes, you will get your product onto the market faster and at a lower cost. And if you involve your customers in the evaluations too, then you will be focusing on their needs in your development and will be launching truly customer-oriented products. Products that the customer is happy to buy and to recommend to others.

25. Marketing communications for real customers

In a survey I conducted, 50 % of those asked think that marketing communications are comprehensible and convincing. But that leaves a further 50 % who are not satisfied with what marketing delivers. I'd like to put a question to you – who is responsible for marketing communications? Who supplies the key information to those in the marketing department concerning your customers, their needs and the problems which the new product is solving for them?

I have a short story to tell on this theme:

In December 2015, I wanted to buy a digital camera at the beginning of my holiday. I went to three different shops and thought I would be able to make up my mind pretty quickly. Then I saw the following information printed in the product description:

"Lithium ion rechargeable battery EN-EL19, mains adapter with battery charging function EH-71P, USB cable UC-E21, maximum aperture f/3.3-5.9."

There I was, in a genuine Bohemian village. There was no one to offer me advice and I wasn't allowed to try out the cameras. None of the three shops got my custom.

Make sure your marketing communications are better than this and take into consideration the information requirements of the customer, the problem you are solving for them and their level of knowledge, so that the customer will be able to understand what you say about the product and its benefits. Your goal is to sell the product and not to place technical details in the foreground.

I recently saw a very successful Huawei advertisement in print:

"Because you have lots of plans for your holidays. The Huawei P9 Plus – with the Leica Dual Camera for high-contrast holiday photos. Get your "Leica to go" – for professional photos without having to carry your camera around with you."

We can assume from this advert that they spoke to their customers and they have solved the following problems for them:

- high-contrast photos
- professional level of quality
- lightweight and easy format which is easy to carry around

No features are named; instead we are given precise information on the things an amateur photographer understands and is looking for.

The following exercise will only take twenty minutes and will provide you with some new findings on your own communications. Find some of your current marketing communications material and analyse it for customer-focused marketing:

- technical language, use cases, powerful words, benefits
- required level of knowledge – layperson, professional
- frequency of use – seldom, occasionally, often
- user problems of the customer
- expectations in terms of information needed

Did you get an immediate understanding of the benefits and added value the product will bring for the customer? No? Then you have gained a better appreciation of how difficult it is for a sales representative to sell products which have been marketed in this way.

26. A Framework for product launches

by Eduardo Lopes

Those who make investments are hoping to achieve a return on their investment. This applies in both our private lives and in business. Companies invest in the development of new products which will ideally sell well and thus bring higher returns than if the money was simply sitting in the bank or was used in any other way.

A product that is in line with the needs of the market will not necessarily be successful, however. It first needs to have its presence

on the market publicised through a carefully planned product launch. Studies have shown that an inadequate product launch can make a significant contribution to the failure of a product and—in the worst case—the failure of the entire company. A carefully planned product launch will inspire customer acceptance for the new product and help it to become quickly established on the market – and will also support the achievement of the desired return on investment.

Although product launches will vary according to the industry, the company and product, good planning, the right level of quality and continuous monitoring of the success of the product life cycle from the start can have a very positive effect.

Table 10 – Overview of the three elements which form the framework for a product launch

Planning	Quality	Measurement of success
Introduction Communications Setting goals	Communications concept Events Launch material	Tracker Actual v. target measurement

Planning the product launch

Running in parallel to product development, a project plan for the product launch will already be in the development stages. This will include the planning of milestones, the communications concept, the definition of marketing goals, staff planning and all the activities surrounding the planning of events, e.g. teaser, e-mails, newsletters, videos, customer events. The ongoing involvement of all stakeholders in this process forms the basis for the required support in the company and thereby for the success of the product. The product launch plan serves as a reference point for the various stakeholders involved in the planning of their respective tasks. It creates an additional level of transparency and understanding for the various activities involved. A product launch plan which has been successfully worked through can then serve as a template for further product launches, thus reducing the amount of work required when products are launched on to the market in the future.

A product launch is like a project in itself. Good product launch planning helps to improve communications and the planning of resources and deadlines. These in turn will help to keep stress levels to a minimum in the end spurt before the actual day of the product launch.

Quality of the product launch

A product launch can be said to be of high quality when the required information is communicated in a straightforward way. The effort required to provide information in a customer-friendly way will pay off in terms of increased advisory expertise, fewer queries and satisfied customers. These effects can be assured with an appropriate communications concept, customer-focused product launch events and the timely provision of the necessary paperwork.

In order to successfully launch a new product onto the

market, both internal and external activities are required. These can be summarised in a communications concept, as follows:

- Activities and responsibilities
- Duration of the launch activities
- Starting point of the launch
- Methods of communications such as flyers, white papers, e-mail marketing campaigns, sales materials
- Sites for communications activities, e.g. trade fairs, trade journals, website
- Testimonials
- Training and training materials
- Planning of support
- PR

A product launch event is organised to present the product to a wider public for the first time. Ideally, this should first of all take place within the company, before the innovation is presented to the market, so that amendments can if necessary be made to the way it is presented. For all of the events surrounding the product launch, it is essential that the focus is on the product and that enough time has been allowed for participants to really get an understanding of the product. As well as being a venue for knowledge transfer, the events should also be fun, as positive experiences tend to stay in our memories. The choice of a special venue for the event, a varied agenda, an impressive accompanying programme or an interesting guest speaker will all have a positive impact on the launch.

Generally speaking, the phrase "face-to-face makes the race" applies here. The physical participation in an event does of course use more resources, but it also has a more long-lasting effect – the potential customer can experience all aspects of the product and there are often also discussions on the product which have a beneficial effect too.

The internal product presentation ensures that the new knowledge is in place within the company to be able to provide optimal support for the sales and distribution of the product, from customer advice through to after-sales support. It is a good idea to involve employees from a broad range of departments in the product launch – in-house sales as well as the field sales force, marketing, product management and support. This will foster acceptance of the new knowledge and will have a positive effect on sales figures. Sales staff who have established knowledge of the product will give more effective presentations than sales employees for whom it is unfamiliar. In addition to the above, hands-on trainings, workshops on product positioning, case studies and quizzes have also proven to be effective. They bring a lively atmosphere to the event and ensure that the new material is firmly embedded in the minds of the participants.

Companies who try to scrimp and save on the internal presentation will find with hindsight that they experience a lack of identification with the product on the part of their employees, as well as a lack of expertise when it comes to advising customers and providing support.

An effective method of presenting the product to external stakeholders is through a press conference or at a trade show. It makes sense at this point to aim at reaching a large number of potential customers. It is thus vital to put in effort at an early stage to get customers to attend the presentations. Stakeholders often have very full diaries and need to be able to make plans well in advance. "Don't do things in half-measures" as the saying goes. "Do things well and talk about it" – to potential customers and at the locations where customers are likely to be found. A company needs to succeed in getting the participants talking about their product afterwards.

Good documentation is helpful as a means of backing up the product launch. This includes, for example:

- presentations
- information sheets
- price lists
- comparisons with the competition
- brochures
- samples
- product films
- photos

The paperwork required should be tailored to the needs of the sales representatives, the support team and the buyers, so that each of them receives the information they need.

Measuring the success of the product launch

Every product launch costs money for the production of the materials and for the launch events. In order that you can pick up on any deviation from the sales plan at an early stage, the monitoring of the product launch is important for the management of success. You will have set out performance indicators for this in good time with the various stakeholders from sales, application, customer service and marketing.

It is often the case that only sales turnover, margin or sales figures are used as measurable parameters. These performance indicators include data from the past. However, it is only possible to react once a deviation already exists. By setting activity-related goals, the success of the product launch can be influenced in advance; for example, by the definition of threshold values for the number of

- offers
- product presentations
- contracts drawn up per customer visit
- enquiries from interested parties
- trade fair stands
- leads

For every performance indicator, threshold values will be needed which lead to previously defined measures being actioned in the case that there is either a shortfall or the value is exceeded. Normally, those responsible for sales and for the product have these performance indicators available to them as a so-called 'tracker', e.g. in the form of a dashboard, CRM or Excel sheets.

Conclusion

The launch of a product is just as important as product development itself. It needs to be comprehensively planned at an early stage so that all stakeholders are involved. Providing information well in advance will make it easier for you to achieve the marketing and sales goals which have been set. Remember, it's important to tell the world about what you are doing. With a well-planned product launch, it is much more likely that a product will be successful.

27. Marketing for Generation Y

In chapter 15, you learned that members of Generation Y require a different style of management, that they function differently. It may be that we need to communicate different messages to this generation and offer new services to them. In a study carried out by Technomar, entitled 'The impact of Generation Y on German businesses', it was established that 28% of companies have recorded a marked decrease in revenues with Generation Y. Losses of revenue of between 19% and 53% mean that new measures are required in marketing communications, both in the B2B and the B2C sectors.

Assuming that your product fulfils customer needs, then you can find some new approaches in this chapter to help your sales department to do better in reaching Generation Y:

- Flexible subscriptions
- Interaction on social media, such as comments, tests,

competitions
- Immediate availability of information and pictures of components
- Regular and transparent communication about the company
- Recommendation marketing for personal networks
- Exclusive information via sneak previews and videos about new products
- Advertising via smartphone
- Various different payment functions via smartphone, bank card and other options

If you are already experiencing a downturn in sales revenues with this target group, then it would be worth carrying out some interviews with individuals from Generation Y. Find out what you could be doing better in terms of product design, marketing communications and sales.

Bibliography and list of source references

Steven Haines 'MANAGING PRODUCT MANAGEMENT', MC Graw Hill, 2012

Herbert Lippmann, Annette Orth 'Mit Produktmanagement Markt-chancen nutzen', published by Wissenschaft & Praxis, 2008, 9th edition

Friedrich Glasl, 'Konfliktmanagement. Ein Handbuch für Führungskräfte, Beraterinnen und Berater', 10th reworked edition, Bern/Stuttgart, 2011

Frank Lemser, Handout 'Technisches Produktmanagement', 2016, certifed training according to the Open Product Management Workflow™: www.proproduktmanagement.de

Ulrike Laubner, 'Fitness-Training für Produktmanager', Bod publishing house, 2014, 2nd edition

Alexander Markowetz, 'Digitaler Burnout', Droemer Knaur, October 2015

Kristian Kunert und Markus Knill, 'Team und Kommunikation', Sauerländer publishing house AG, 2nd editions, 2000

Andreas Ebneter: 'Erfolgreich in der ersten Chefposition' published by PRAXIUM, Zurich, 2007

Rahn, Horst-Joachim, 'Erfolgreiche Teamführung', Windmühle, publishing house, Hamburg, 2010

Martin Blatter, Fabia Hartwagner, 'Digitale Lehr- und Lernbegleiter", 1st edition, hep publishing house AG, Bern

Roman Diehl, 'Klischées über die Generation Y gehen an der Realität vorbei', ConsultingCumLaude, 2014

R. Wagner, M. Wittmann, S. Ries, 'Vorsicht vor Stereotypen- Was die Generation Y motiviert', 'Wirtschaftspsychologie aktuell', edition 3/2012

Andreas Varesi, 'Studie zu Auswirkungen der Generation Y auf die deutschen Unternehmer', Technomar GmbH, June 2013

N.F. Taylor, 'Marketing to Millenials: How to capture GenY Consumers', Business News Daily, 15.6.2014

Carl R. Rogers, 'Der neue Mensch', Klett-Cotta, 10th edition, 2015

Eduardo Lopes, 'Reach the market! Analyse des globalen Produkte- Launch Ansatzes von SealedAir, Diversey Care für Bodenreinigungsmaschinen', Diploma thesis 2014

Dr. T. Mandel, Dr. R. Fuchs, M. Rauch, L Commolli, C. Forestier D. Wallmer 'Swiss Product Management 2013/2014: Von den Besten lernen', Zurich University of the Applied Sciences, 2014

Planview® INC., Fourth benchmark study on Product Portfolio Management, 'Der Zustand der Produktentwicklung in 2013', 2013

Actinium Consulting, 'Fachbereichsverantwortliche vertrauen zunehmend den Analysen der BI-Systemen', March 2013

Marike Frick 'Tanz mit mir', 'Die Zeit', 25th October 2012

Mobility Coach, Lifelong Learning Programme, 'Theorie der non- verbalen Kommunikation", DE/12/LLp-LdV/TOI/147 151

Prof. Dr Dietmar Kremmel, 'Wirksames Produktmanagement als Schlüssel zum Erfolg', 'KMU-Magazin', Number 1, February 2008

Mathias Pöhm, 'VIP Rhetorik exklusiv', Handout, 2014

C.A. Di Bendetto, 'Identifying the Key Success Factors in New Product Launch', 'Prod. Innovation Management', 1999, S. 530- 544

J.P. Guiltian, 'Launch Strategy, Launch Tactics, and Demand Outcome', 'Journal of Product Innovation Management', edition 16, November 1999, S. 502-529

E. Hultink, A. Griffin, S. Hart, H.S. Robben, 'Identifying the Key Success Factors in New Product Launch performance', Prod Innov Management, 1997, pages 243-257

Y. Lee, G. Colarelli O'Conner, 'New Product Launch Strategy for

Network Effects Products', 'Journal of the Academy of Marketing Science', edition 31, 2003, page 241-255

R. Lombriser, P.A. Abplanalp, 'Strategisches Management', Versus publishing house AG, Zurich, 2010

K. Pauwels, J. Silva-Risso, S. Srinivasan, D.M. Hanssens, D. M.,

'New Products, Sales Promotions and Firm Value: The case of the automobile industry', Journal of Marketing, October 2014, pages 142ffSchneider & Associates, 'New product launch report', Boston, http://www.schneiderpr.com, 2015